LET'S DISCUSS

PERSONAL SAFETY

Pete Sanders and Steve Myers

Watts Books

LONDON • SYDNEY

© Aladdin Books Ltd 1995

Designed and produced by
Aladdin Books Ltd
28 Percy Street
London W1P 0LD

First published in
Great Britain in 1995 by
Watts Books
96 Leonard Street
London EC2A 4RH
Reprinted 1997

ISBN: 0 7496 2191 5

A catalogue record for this
book is available from the
British Library.

Printed in Belgium

Designer   Tessa Barwick
Editor   Sarah Levete
Illustrator   Mike Lacey
Picture research Brooks
                 Krikler
                 Research

Pete Sanders is Senior
Lecturer in health education
at the University of North
London. He was a head
teacher for ten years and has
written many books on social
issues for children.

Steve Myers is a freelance
writer. He has co-written
other titles in this series and
worked on several educational
projects for children.

The consultant, Pam Nicholls,
is a Senior Project Worker
with the Children's Society.

Contents

HOW TO USE THIS BOOK

The books in this series are intended to help young people to understand more about personal issues that may affect their lives. Each book can be read alone, or together with a parent, carer, teacher or helper, so that there is an opportunity to talk through ideas as they come up. Issues raised in the storyline are explored in the accompanying text, inviting further discussion.

At the end of the book there is a chapter called "What Can We Do?". This section provides practical ideas which will be useful for both young people and adults, as well as a list of the names and addresses of organisations and helplines, which offer further information and support.

−1− Introduction

Everybody has the right to feel safe. Some of the responsibility for this lies with other people. However, there is a lot we can do for ourselves to make sure that we stay safe.

In order to protect yourself, you need to be aware of the ways in which your safety might be put at risk. Knowing about the possible dangers puts you in a better position to avoid problems. This book explains what being safe means, looks at some of the threats to our security, and discusses what can be done about them. Each chapter introduces a different aspect of the subject, illustrated by a continuing storyline. The characters in the story deal with situations which many young people experience. By the end you will understand more about the importance of personal safety.

—2— What We Mean By Safety

At first, we look to our parents or carers to protect us. As we grow up, we take on more responsibility for our own safety.

Safety is one of life's basic needs. To many people, safety simply means the absence of danger. However, personal safety is not only about avoiding or preventing physical risks to your health. It is also concerned with your emotional and social well-being. How you feel about yourself and the world around you is just as important as being in a safe physical environment. As you grow older, you begin to discover what is safe and what is not.

Sometimes we learn through experience. For instance, a small child may touch something hot and so find out that it can burn and is painful. He or she will be unlikely to do this again! Often other people tell you about dangers, and you start to understand the risks of a particular situation, without having to experience them for yourself.

Every person has a different idea of safety and danger. Some may feel no fear if they look down from a tall building, but others may be terrified. Dangers to our security are often presented in an exaggerated way, such as fantasy monsters. But in reality, threats to our safety are more ordinary. With common sense many of these can be avoided.

Sometimes an imagined fear or danger can be as frightening as a real danger.

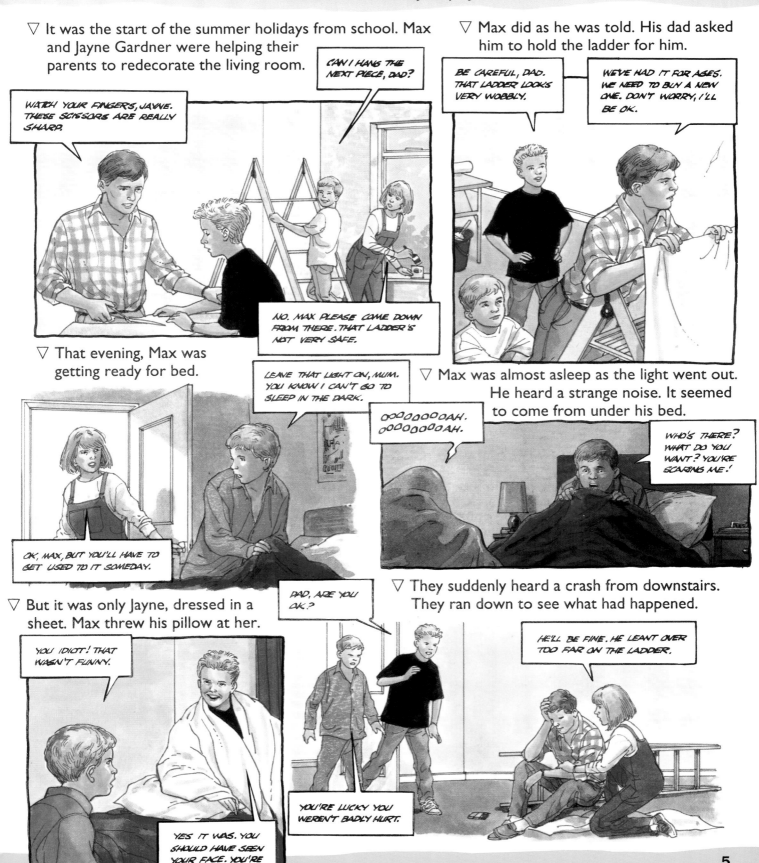

△ It was the start of the summer holidays from school. Max and Jayne Gardner were helping their parents to redecorate the living room.

CAN I HANG THE NEXT PIECE, DAD?

WATCH YOUR FINGERS, JAYNE. THESE SCISSORS ARE REALLY SHARP.

NO. MAX PLEASE COME DOWN FROM THERE. THAT LADDER'S NOT VERY SAFE.

△ Max did as he was told. His dad asked him to hold the ladder for him.

BE CAREFUL, DAD. THAT LADDER LOOKS VERY WOBBLY.

WE'VE HAD IT FOR AGES. WE NEED TO BUY A NEW ONE. DON'T WORRY, I'LL BE OK.

△ That evening, Max was getting ready for bed.

LEAVE THAT LIGHT ON, MUM. YOU KNOW I CAN'T GO TO SLEEP IN THE DARK.

OK, MAX, BUT YOU'LL HAVE TO GET USED TO IT SOMEDAY.

△ Max was almost asleep as the light went out. He heard a strange noise. It seemed to come from under his bed.

OOOOOOOOAH. OOOOOOOOAH.

WHO'S THERE? WHAT DO YOU WANT? YOU'RE SCARING ME!

△ But it was only Jayne, dressed in a sheet. Max threw his pillow at her.

YOU IDIOT! THAT WASN'T FUNNY.

YES IT WAS. YOU SHOULD HAVE SEEN YOUR FACE. YOU'RE SUCH A BABY, BEING AFRAID OF THE DARK.

△ They suddenly heard a crash from downstairs. They ran down to see what had happened.

DAD, ARE YOU OK?

HE'LL BE FINE. HE LEANT OVER TOO FAR ON THE LADDER.

YOU'RE LUCKY YOU WEREN'T BADLY HURT.

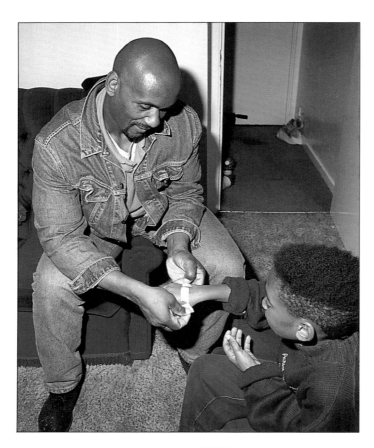

THE WORD 'ACCIDENT' MEANS SOMETHING UNEXPECTED, HAPPENING BY CHANCE.

An accident might be the result of taking unnecessary risks, or failing to take simple precautions. Or it may be that the person is unaware of the danger, or simply thinks "it won't happen to me". With a little more care, Mr Gardner could have avoided falling off the ladder.

IMAGINED DANGERS CAN SEEM VERY REAL.

Jayne has scared Max by pretending to be a ghost. Being able to tell the difference between situations where there is an actual risk to your safety, and those in which the danger is in your mind, is important. Recognising this can help to avoid possible problems and prevents unnecessary anxiety.

CASE STUDY:
CHARLIE, AGED 12

"I used to be terrified of the dark. I'd imagine all sorts of monsters and things hiding in the shadows. I couldn't sleep without a light by my bed. Although people said it was silly, I was still scared. One night, I decided to try to sleep without the light on. I was frightened at first. My eyes could make out shapes in the dark, but I kept telling myself that they were just furniture and toys. It was much easier than I'd thought. After a few nights, I was used to it. It was OK."

— 3 — Safety Around The Home

Did you know that most accidents happen at home? Did you also know that most of them could be avoided?

Most of us assume that our home is a place where we can feel comfortable and protected. Because it is the one place where we expect to feel safe and secure, we often forget to take precautions which could help prevent accidents at home. It is important not to take home safety for granted. Everybody has a part to play; we all have a responsibility to help each other and ourselves.

Some of the ways in which you can make sure you are safe around the house may seem obvious, but are sometimes easy to forget. For instance, you should never go near electrical equipment with water or other liquids – doing so could be very dangerous. Many pieces of furniture have sharp edges and corners on which you could hurt yourself if you run around inside the house. It is not a good idea to play near mirrors, windows or glass doors.

Fires in the home can be a particular hazard. They are easily caused by someone accidentally dropping a lighted cigarette or match, or by an accident in the kitchen.

Some homes have been specifically designed with safety in mind for young, elderly or disabled people. It is worth taking a look around the house, and thinking about ways in which you could help to make sure your home is safe for you, your family and anyone who visits.

Games can cause accidents to furniture, but there is also a risk to the physical safety of young people.

▽ The following weekend, Max went round to play at his friend Anton's house.

YOU WON'T CATCH ME!

WOULD YOU TWO SLOW DOWN! YOU'RE GOING TO HURT YOURSELVES.

▽ They ignored him. Max and Anton rushed into the kitchen and began to play fight.

ANTON! STOP THAT RIGHT NOW. YOU NEARLY SENT THAT SAUCEPAN FLYING.

SORRY, MRS MILNE. WE WERE ONLY PLAYING.

I'VE TOLD ANTON A MILLION TIMES - THIS IS A KITCHEN, NOT A PLAYGROUND. IT'S TOO DANGEROUS TO BE MESSING AROUND.

△ Mrs Milne said they could run about in the garden.

▷ Max pretended to shoot. He hadn't realised that the drill was plugged in. The drill cut his hand.

▽ Instead, the boys went into the garage.

HEY, LOOK AT THIS. COME ANY CLOSER AND I'LL SHOOT.

BE CAREFUL WITH THAT, MAX.

WHAT'S ALL THE SHOUTING ABOUT? WHAT ON EARTH ARE YOU TWO DOING IN HERE?

MAX HAS CUT HIMSELF, DAD. IT LOOKS QUITE DEEP.

▽ Mr Milne took Max inside and cleaned and dressed the wound. He was very angry with the two boys.

YOU'RE LUCKY IT WAS ONLY A SMALL CUT. IT LOOKED WORSE THAN IT WAS. THOSE THINGS ARE NOT TOYS, YOU KNOW. YOU HAD NO BUSINESS BEING IN THERE.

I'M REALLY SORRY, MR MILNE. I DIDN'T MEAN ANY HARM.

WELL, TO KEEP YOU BOYS OUT OF TROUBLE, YOU CAN BOTH GO UPSTAIRS AND CLEAR UP ANTON'S ROOM.

MAX HAS HURT HIMSELF, PLAYING WITH THE DRILL.

It is important to remember that not everything is a toy. Many young people have been injured because they have not been aware of the risk, or because they have misused things. You may think your actions are harmless, but you could be putting yourself and other people in danger.

ANTON AND MAX HAVE BEEN SENT TO TIDY UP ANTON'S ROOM.

Like them, you may think that tidying up can be boring and unnecessary. But putting things away in their proper place is an effective way of preventing accidents. You may know where everything is, but someone else could easily slip or trip over toys, computer equipment or video games which may have been left on the floor. Avoid leaving electrical flexes stretched over spaces where people might walk. Items left on the stairs can be particularly dangerous.

FACT FILE: KITCHEN SAFETY

- Hot surfaces do not always look hot. Never leave paper or tea towels near the cooker. Tie back long hair and roll up loose sleeves if you are cooking.
- Pan handles should always be turned inwards to the cooker, otherwise they may be knocked. Make sure they are not over a flame or heat. Kettle flexes etc. should not be left dangling, as these can be caught accidentally.
- Always use knives and scissors with care. Put them away safely and carefully.
- Bleaches and other cleaning items are often kept in the kitchen. They are very poisonous.

4

Outdoor Safety

"We were messing around in this building site. It was fun at first but Jamie cut himself on some metal. We couldn't get out. Nobody could hear us shouting for help."

Most people are aware of some of the ways in which they can keep themselves safe outside. You have probably been told to take care on roads, or when you are near water. You will know not to talk to strangers, or to take anything from them. There are many other ways in which you can take responsibility for your safety and well-being when you are outdoors.

Although it can be tempting to play in places like building sites or derelict houses, they are often full of potential dangers.

Understanding the environment is important. Weather conditions can change very quickly. Remember that protecting yourself from too much sun is as important as proper clothing in 'bad' weather. Wearing the right clothes for the conditions and for the activity you are involved in will help to protect you. At night, for instance, bright colours are easily visible.

Being sensible about where you choose to play, and knowing that dangers may not be immediately obvious, will help avoid problems. Young people have ignored warnings and have been injured and killed playing on railways or electricity pylons. There are many other places where you can enjoy yourself, without putting yourself and others at risk.

▽ Towards the end of the school holidays, Max and Jayne went to stay with their cousin, Ryan, and his step-sister, Adele.

▽ They set off for the beach. Jayne hadn't brought her bike, and rode with Ryan.

▽ Everyone swerved. Ryan and Jayne were thrown from their bike and landed on the grass at the side of the road.

△ All three bikes were level as they came round the corner.

▽ The man said that at least nobody was hurt, and he drove away.

△ They spent a couple of hours on the beach. Then Ryan suggested they go exploring.

▽ Adele hadn't realised how strong the currents were. She was suddenly too far out, and in difficulty.

▽ Adele had to swim to safety. She went to find the others but they were already on their way back to the beach and missed her.

MAYBE SHE JUST DECIDED TO GO HOME.

SHE MUST HAVE DONE. COME ON, LET'S GET BACK. I'M STARVING.

▽ Adele was not at home when they got there. She arrived ten minutes later, very upset.

WHY ON EARTH DID YOU GO OFF LIKE THAT? ANYTHING COULD HAVE HAPPENED. HOW MANY TIMES HAVE I TOLD YOU YOU SHOULD ALWAYS STAY TOGETHER, ESPECIALLY BY THE WATER?

WE THOUGHT SHE'D BE OK.

WELL I WASN'T. YOU JUST LEFT ME.

▽ Adele's dad offered Adele a burger from the barbecue.

COME ON, EAT SOMETHING. AT LEAST THERE'S NO HARM DONE.

I DON'T WANT ONE OF THOSE. THEY'RE TOO FATTY. I'LL JUST HAVE SOME SALAD. AND YOU SHOULDN'T SMOKE WHEN YOU'RE DOING THAT.

▽ Adele's dad put his cigarette in the ash-tray. Suddenly it blew off and landed in some grass.

QUICKLY, PUT IT OUT. THE GRASS IS REALLY DRY AROUND HERE.

IT'S OK, PANIC OVER. IT'S OUT.

COME ON, I THINK WE SHOULD GET SOME FOOD BEFORE ANYTHING ELSE HAPPENS TODAY!

△ Laughing, they all went over to get some food.

WATER IS FUN BUT IT CAN ALSO BE HAZARDOUS.

As Adele has discovered, it is important to know the depth of water, and to understand how strong currents can be. Water in ponds or canals can be very dirty, and may contain objects which could cause injury. Always follow the safety rules in a swimming pool. Learning to swim will help to keep you safe near water.

PLAYING WITH FIRE OR FIREWORKS IS VERY DANGEROUS.

Fires can cause terrible damage to people and property. Never stand too close to a fire, whether or not there is a flame, and keep sleeves and other parts of clothing well-clear. Materials can burn very easily. In some countries, huge areas of land have been destroyed because a match or cigarette has been carelessly thrown away.

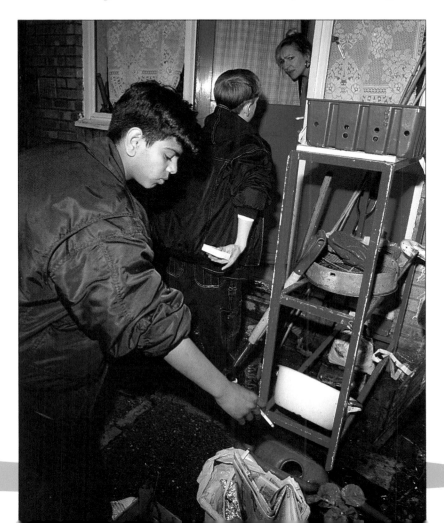

FACT FILE:
ROAD SAFETY

- Always cross the road at a safe point, such as a pedestrian crossing.
- Avoid crossing from between parked cars, or other positions where you and the traffic can't see each other properly.
- Always look around carefully before you cross. Make sure you have correctly judged the distance and speed of the traffic.
- If there is no pavement, always walk facing oncoming traffic, so that you can step to the side of the road in good time.
- With young children, make sure they walk on the inside of the pavement, and that they hold your hand when crossing.
- Always wear a protective helmet when cycling and always follow the highway code.
- At night, wear light coloured clothing and/or reflective strips.
- Never play in the road.

Emotional Safety

5

It is often easier to know how to protect ourselves against dangers to our physical safety than to deal with those which pose a threat to our emotional security. But just as there are practical measures we can take to avoid physical injury, there are also ways of looking after our emotional well-being. Feeling safe emotionally involves learning how to cope with, express and safeguard your feelings. This means developing your sense of self-worth and respect for other people. It includes making carefully considered choices and decisions which will affect your life.

"Nobody realised what was happening. They all thought I was fine. For ages I was too scared and felt too ashamed to tell anyone that I was being bullied."

It is important to learn how to stand up for yourself, without being aggressive.

Sometimes, people forget how essential their feelings are to their well-being. Expressing them is not always easy. It may be difficult to find the right words to describe a particular emotion or it may be difficult to admit to others to feeling a certain way. However, support from others enables us to talk about issues and it helps us to understand how we feel about ourselves and other people.

Unfortunately, people do not always respect other people's feelings. For instance, bullies may deliberately try to make a person feel bad.

Our sense of security is just as important as the knowledge that we are not in immediate danger. If you know that you are safe at the moment, but think that your safety will soon be in danger, the worry that this might cause can be just as serious as the danger itself.

▽ It was the end of the holidays. Jayne was getting ready to go to her new school.

IT WON'T BE THE SAME. WHAT IF NOBODY LIKES ME?

DON'T BE SILLY. OF COURSE THEY WILL. YOU'RE BOUND TO FEEL NERVOUS ON YOUR FIRST DAY, BUT I'M SURE EVERYTHING WILL BE FINE.

▽ Her mum was right. Jayne quickly made lots of new friends. She particularly liked Steph, an older girl.

YOU'RE OK, JAYNE. YOU CAN HANG AROUND WITH US.

YEAH, STEPH'S A GOOD LAUGH.

IT SOUNDS GOOD TO ME.

▽ A few weeks later, Jayne asked her mum if she could have some new trainers.

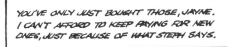

I WANT SOME LIKE STEPH'S. SHE SAYS THAT MINE ARE REALLY OLD-FASHIONED.

STEPH'S ALL YOU EVER TALK ABOUT THESE DAYS.

YOU'VE ONLY JUST BOUGHT THOSE, JAYNE. I CAN'T AFFORD TO KEEP PAYING FOR NEW ONES, JUST BECAUSE OF WHAT STEPH SAYS.

IT WILL BE. ESPECIALLY IF YOU DON'T MIND BREAKING A FEW RULES.

NO, OF COURSE NOT.

△ Jayne wasn't sure what Steph meant, but she liked her.

ALL THE OTHER GIRLS HAVE THEM. YOU DON'T CARE WHAT THEY THINK, DO YOU? IF YOU LOVED ME, YOU'D BUY THEM FOR ME.

▷ Jayne refused to listen. She stormed upstairs to her room.

JAYNE, THAT'S A TERRIBLE THING TO SAY. IT'S TOTALLY UNFAIR, AND YOU KNOW IT.

WHAT IS THE MATTER WITH HER LATELY? SHE SEEMS LIKE A DIFFERENT PERSON SINCE SHE STARTED HANGING ROUND WITH THIS STEPH.

I KNOW. SHE HARDLY EVER WANTS TO PLAY ANY MORE. SHE'S ALWAYS OUT WITH STEPH AND HER FRIENDS.

△ Mrs Gardner was unsure what to do for the best.

MRS GARDNER IS NOT LETTING HERSELF BE INFLUENCED BY WHAT JAYNE HAS SAID.

People can try to manipulate others to make them behave in a certain way. You may know people who have said they won't be your friend unless you do what they want. Although both young people and adults are capable of behaving in this way, it can create tension and conflict between people.

RELATIONSHIPS AFFECT HOW WE FEEL ABOUT OURSELVES.

Relationships are important in our lives but making friends is not always easy. Sometimes people pretend to be something they are not, in order to be liked. This does not help to build good friendships.

JAYNE IS CONVINCED THAT SHE IS NOT GOING TO ENJOY HER NEW SCHOOL.

The outlook people have on a situation can affect what happens, and how they are treated. Someone who assumes the worst may think they are protecting themselves from disappointment by assuming things will go wrong. However, having a positive attitude can mean enjoying and appreciating situations and people more. Jealousy, or always thinking that what other people have is better than what you have, can make you feel very unhappy. Rather than bottling up your feelings, it helps to discuss them with someone.

6

Risk-taking And Dares

"I was late, but catching the bus would have meant running out into traffic. It wasn't worth the risk."

To take a risk means to do something where there is a chance that the outcome might not be what you want or expect. A dare is a challenge from one person to another. It will usually involve some form of risk-taking. Although there is a sense of adventure and fun in taking risks, it can pose a threat to your safety. Having fun or being adventurous doesn't mean you have to take risks.

People take risks every day. For some they make life more exciting. Not all risks involve physical danger. It might be a case of changing jobs or moving house, without being totally sure whether it is the right thing to do. Often people will take what is called a 'calculated' risk. This means that they have carefully thought about the possible outcomes and have tried to lessen the chances of anything going wrong. Some people, however, do not think through the consequences of their actions. They act on the spur of the moment, or because they are being pressured into doing so.

You do not have to give in to a dare. Doing something dangerous because someone tells you to does not make you a braver or better person. Standing up for yourself and saying no will make other people respect you more. It will also make you feel more confident about yourself.

There are ways of enjoying yourself without taking unnecessary risks. For instance, wearing a helmet when skateboarding will help to protect you.

▽ The following Sunday, Max was playing with Anton and another friend, Ben.

▽ Jayne met Steph and the girls in an abandoned warehouse.

▽ Lucy wanted to give up, but daren't. She suddenly lost her footing and fell from the girder.

▽ Max thought about everything he had learned about smoking from his parents and his teachers.

▽ Lucy was going to try to walk from one side of the warehouse to the other on a narrow girder.

▽ Jayne and Steph began to argue.

AS LUCY AND JAYNE HAVE DISCOVERED, BEING PART OF A GANG CAN GET OUT OF HAND.

Gang members may dare each other to do things which are dangerous or illegal, or both. You may be afraid of being called a coward if you do not go along with everyone else. But refusing to take part, if you think an action is wrong, is a brave and responsible choice. Being part of a group can be fun without being dangerous.

SOMETIMES YOU MAY FEEL PRESSURE TO EXPERIMENT WITH SUBSTANCES SUCH AS DRUGS OR ALCOHOL.

These can be dangerous, and both will damage your ability to look after yourself. Although trying some new things can be enjoyable and is part of growing up, you should never feel you have to do anything which might put you at risk.

CASE STUDY: ANNIE, AGED 14

"I used to hang around with a group of friends. They dared me to steal from the local shop. I did it because I didn't want to look a fool in front of everybody else, and I wanted them to like me. But I felt so guilty about it. The next time someone dared me, I said no. A few of the others made fun of me at first, but afterwards some of them said they felt the same way I did. I felt good that I had stood up for myself."

7

Dangers From Other People

Although you can take some responsibility for your own well-being, it is important to be aware how the actions of other people can also affect your safety.

Accidents and other threats to your safety may sometimes be caused by other people's lack of thought, or by their neglecting to take action. Most people have no desire to be violent or to hurt other people. Unfortunately, from time to time, you will hear of somebody who deliberately sets out to harm others. Some people's behaviour can put others in great danger.

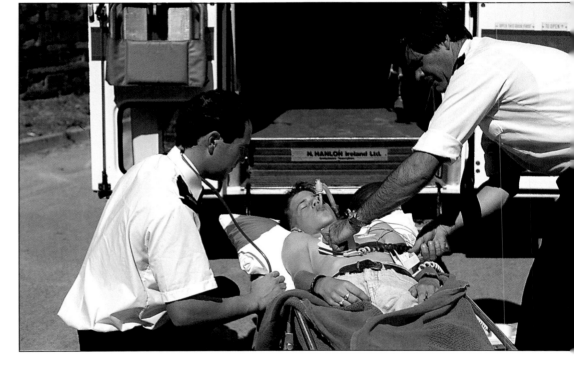

People who drive when they have drunk too much alcohol or taken illegal drugs can cause serious accidents to other people.

Some people put others in danger because they are not thinking clearly or considerately. Others do not seem to care how their actions affect other people. For instance, joy riders show no consideration for their own safety or that of others. There are laws and rules to prevent this kind of behaviour. Health and safety regulations are enforced in companies and public buildings, such as schools. These help to reduce the number of accidents and cut down on work which is not up to standard. People have caused accidents because they are not qualified, or because they are too tired, to do a task properly.

▽ Over the next few weeks, Steph began to bully Jayne.

▽ Steph stepped aside. As Jayne walked past, Steph put her foot out and tripped her up.

△ Jayne had become more and more unhappy as the bullying continued.

▽ One evening, Max was late leaving Anton's house. He thought about taking a short cut.

▽ Max hurried away. He ran all the way home.

▽ Max told his dad about the stranger.

MAX WAS RIGHT NOT TO ACCEPT THE LIFT.
Not all strangers are a threat, but it is sensible to be cautious. You should never accept a lift from or go off with a stranger, even if the person claims to know you or your family or if you know them only slightly – for example, someone you have talked to in a shop or have met at a friend's house.

EVERYBODY HAS THE RIGHT TO BE SAFE.
But there are people who deliberately harm young people. If you know of some-one who is being abused, or if you are being abused yourself, talk to someone you trust about it, however hard this is.

FACT FILE: BULLYING

- All bullying is wrong.
- Bullying is not the action of a brave person.
- Bullying can take different forms – from threats and name-calling to actual violence.
- Nobody deserves to be bullied.
- Bullying can make people feel very unhappy.
- Most people recognise that bullying is unacceptable. Many schools treat the problem very seriously.
- Bullies rely on people not telling on them.
- Standing up for yourself can sometimes stop bullying. Or, if you are being bullied or see that someone else is being bullied, talk to an adult who can help – perhaps a parent or a teacher.

– 8 – Other People And Safety

We can all take steps to protect ourselves. Other people can and do help us in this. The emergency services – police, fire brigade and ambulance – are obvious ways in which other people are concerned with our safety. Very young children and babies, who are not aware of the risks, are often dependent on older people to protect them and to teach them about safety.

Other people may need our help to keep them safe. This is why it is important for us all to take safety seriously, not only in what we say, but also in what we do.

Nearly everything that we buy from shops has been approved for safety. Medicines are tested before they are allowed to be sold or prescribed. Products have instructions for use which are important to read because they have been written to protect you from possible harm as a result of misuse.

If you don't immediately understand a rule, it is worth remembering that it is there for a purpose. However, safety messages do not always agree with each other. For instance, some people believe that violence on TV and in films encourages young people to take dangerous risks. Others disagree.

▽ A month later, Jayne ran into Steph and her boyfriend.

WELL, LOOK WHO IT IS. WHAT DO YOU THINK YOU'RE LOOKING AT?

SORRY, I DIDN'T KNOW IT WAS YOU.

WHO'S THIS? IS THIS THE ONE YOU WERE TELLING ME ABOUT?

YES. LOOK AT HER FACE. I THINK SHE'S JEALOUS OF US. SHE KNOWS SHE'LL NEVER HAVE A BOYFRIEND.

WHY DO YOU HAVE TO BE SO HORRIBLE?

△ Jayne walked home feeling miserable.

▽ Eventually, Jayne told her mum everything.

IT FEELS GOOD TO TALK IT THROUGH WITH SOMEONE. YOU SHOULD HAVE SEEN STEPH AND HER BOYFRIEND KISSING!

IT SOUNDS TO ME LIKE STEPH'S TRYING TO GROW UP TOO QUICKLY. SHE MIGHT END UP REGRETTING IT. WOULD YOU LIKE ME TO TALK TO THE SCHOOL ABOUT BULLYING?

▽ Mrs Gardner could tell something was wrong.

WON'T YOU TELL ME WHAT'S WRONG? YOU'VE BEEN UNHAPPY FOR WEEKS NOW. IS IT STEPH? ARE YOU UPSET ABOUT FALLING OUT WITH HER?

YOU DON'T NORMALLY LOOK SO HAPPY ABOUT YOUR DAY AT SCHOOL.

A POLICEMAN CAME IN TO CLASS TODAY. WE TALKED ABOUT SAFETY AND THE THINGS WE CAN DO TO LOOK OUT FOR EACH OTHER. IT WAS REALLY INTERESTING.

I REALISED I KNEW QUITE A LOT OF IT ALREADY. SOME OF IT'S JUST COMMON SENSE.

▷ Jayne said she wanted to handle it herself. Max came in from school.

24

JAYNE HAS FOUND IT HAS HELPED HER TO TALK TO HER MUM ABOUT STEPH.

Discussing a situation can be a useful way of sorting out a problem. Another person's thoughts can help you to understand your own feelings. This is especially true if you cannot decide whether or not to believe what you have been told, or if you are facing pressure from others to behave in a certain way, which you think might be risky.

MRS GARDNER REALISES THAT STEPH IS RUSHING INTO AN INTIMATE RELATIONSHIP WITH HER BOYFRIEND.

There can be a lot of pressure to have a boy-friend or girlfriend, but there is no rule which says you must. Starting an intimate relationship is not something to be taken lightly. There are issues to be considered which might affect your physical and emotional safety and well-being.

CASE STUDY: INDIRA, AGED 11

"It can be confusing sometimes. One person will say one thing about safety and another will say something else. Some of my friends are allowed to do loads of things which my parents would say I'm too young to do. I'm not allowed to watch TV after certain times but at my friend's house I can watch videos. It's often difficult to know what to do for the best. I've been told never to lie or hit somebody, but other times you're told that if someone is threatening you or trying to make you go off with them, then you can make up an excuse or hit them, especially if you're in real danger. I suppose it's a question of thinking it all through, and of deciding what is the best way of coping."

—9— Ways Of Keeping Safe

Being aware of dangers to your physical and emotional well-being is the first step towards protecting yourself. At the same time, it is important to keep everything in perspective. Being over-anxious can itself lead to problems. Remember also that you have a responsibility towards others. Your actions and decisions can affect their safety as well as your own.

Safety depends both on your attitude to it and on outside factors. These may include what time it is, where you are, who else is there.

Many of the ways in which each of us can keep ourself safe are very simple – for example, thinking ahead and knowing what to do in case of an emergency. Knowing that situations can change is also important.

Your safety might also rely on taking notice of what people and signs tell you. Although rules and regulations are sometimes difficult to accept and might seem very restrictive, they are usually there for a good reason.

Parents and carers may make decisions about the time you have to be home, or perhaps they will always want to know exactly where you are going, and who with. They do this because they care about you, and want to know that you are going to be safe.

Keeping to these rules, and letting people know if you are going to be late is a responsible way to behave, and can save a lot of worry.

THE ICE IS TOO THIN. IT'LL NEVER HOLD HER.

I KNOW. STEPH, THAT'S NOT SAFE. YOU COULD GO THROUGH THE ICE.

◁ One afternoon, Max, Anton, Jayne and Lucy went to the park. They bumped into Steph and her friends, playing on the ice.

JAYNE'S RIGHT, STEPH. YOU SHOULD COME OFF THERE.

WHAT DOES SHE KNOW? I'M SICK AND TIRED OF HER GETTING IN MY WAY. SHE NEEDS TO BE TAUGHT A LESSON.

I'M NOT IMPRESSED OR FRIGHTENED. I JUST FIND YOU BORING. I USED TO THINK YOU WERE OK, BUT NOW I'VE SEEN WHAT YOU'RE REALLY LIKE.

IF IT ISN'T LITTLE MISS KNOW ALL, CAREFUL GIRLS, SHE MIGHT BORE YOU TO DEATH.

◁ Steph started to say something, but Jayne turned around and walked away.

I'VE DONE MY BEST TO STAY OUT OF YOUR WAY. I DON'T PARTICULARLY LIKE YOU, STEPH, BUT I DON'T WANT TO SEE YOU HURT. I'M NOT GOING TO BE UPSET BY YOUR THREATS ANYMORE.

▽ The four friends were going home when someone called out to them.

CAN YOU HELP ME, PLEASE? I THINK I'VE TWISTED MY ANKLE.

MUM AND DAD SAID WE SHOULDN'T TALK TO STRANGERS.

▷ The woman could not stand. Lucy and Max made her as comfortable as they could. Jayne and Anton went to phone for an ambulance.

THERE ARE FOUR OF US, MAX. THIS IS DIFFERENT. SHE COULD BE BADLY HURT.

▽ Later that evening, Max and Jayne told their parents about what had happened with Steph and the old lady.

WE WON'T BE LONG. I'LL PHONE MUM, TOO, AND LET HER KNOW WHAT'S HAPPENED.

IT SOUNDS LIKE YOU DID A GREAT JOB. AND YOU WERE VERY SENSIBLE TO STAY TOGETHER, ESPECIALLY IN THE DARK.

THE AMBULANCEWOMAN SAID SHE'D BE FINE. JUST A SPRAINED ANKLE.

CAN YOU PHONE MY DAD, TOO? I PROMISED TO BE HOME BEFORE DARK, BUT I THINK WE SHOULD STAY TOGETHER UNTIL THE AMBULANCE COMES.

I'M GLAD YOU'VE SORTED OUT THE SITUATION WITH STEPH, TOO.

WELL I'M SURE SHE'LL HAVE SOMETHING TO SAY ON MONDAY. SHE'S NOT WORTH WORRYING ABOUT. I'M REALLY GLAD I STOOD UP TO HER.

Every young person has the right to be protected, and to feel physically and emotionally safe and secure.
If you do have any worries about your safety or well-being, talk to an adult who you trust – perhaps a parent, carer or teacher.

VISITORS:

- Always use the door chain or peep-hole, if you have one, to check on the visitor, before letting him or her in. Never open the door unless you are sure who is calling.
- Always ask to see identification, if the person says he or she is representing a company or official service, such as the police or gas board.

EMERGENCIES:

- Make sure you know emergency telephone numbers: police, fire and ambulance services; parents' or carers' work numbers; neighbours' telephone numbers.
- Make sure you always have change to use a public telephone.
- Learn how to make a reverse-charge call in case of emergency.
- Try to remain calm. Explain clearly what the problem is and where help is needed.
- Only make an emergency phone call to the emergency services when essential.

BEING ASSERTIVE:

- Being assertive does not mean being aggressive. It means standing up for yourself in a calm and positive way .
- Say clearly how you feel. Try not to make personal comments about other people.
- Keep your voice calm – do not shout.
- Try not to be provoked into name-calling.
- Learn how to read a situation – if it seems to be getting out of hand, walk away.
- Don't be afraid of saying no.
- Don't be afraid of asking for help from others.

KEEPING HEALTHY AND SAFE:

Keeping fit and eating a balanced diet are important for your health, well-being and personal safety.

• A balanced diet means making sure that you are eating enough of each kind of food – meat and fish, dairy products, fruit and vegetables and bread and cereals.

• If you are a vegetarian, you need to make sure that you are still getting the protein and minerals which you would otherwise eat in meat.

• Regular exercise is good for your body and is enjoyable. It can help to prevent some diseases.

• If you are worried about any aspect of your health, talk to someone you trust about your concerns.

• A knowledge of first aid is very useful, and can sometimes even save lives.

• There are many courses offered which will teach you what to do – and what not to do – in case of burns, cuts, broken bones, etc.

WALKING OR TRAVELLING:

• Always try to walk in groups. Use well-lit streets at night, even if it makes your journey longer. Never accept a lift from someone you do not know well or trust.

• In trains, sit with other people. Change carriages if you feel unsafe at any point.

• If you think you are being followed, cross the road. Stay near other people. Look for someone like a police officer or traffic warden. If you are still worried, knock on a door or try to alert someone's attention.

• If you are going to be in a crowded place with other people, have an arranged meeting place, in case you become separated.

• Always let parents or carers know where you are going and when you expect to be back. If you miss your train or bus, phone home – reverse the charges if necessary.

• Make sure you have the correct equipment and clothing for cycling.

• Always wear a seat belt when travelling in a car or when provided in a coach.

"At first, I was nervous about standing up for myself, but I think my friends respected me more because I spoke out."

Having read this book, you will know some of the ways in which you can protect yourself and others from risk. Being safe doesn't mean that you cannot enjoy yourself. You will understand that personal safety is also to do with how you feel about yourself and others. It is important to protect your emotional safety by learning how to express your emotions and understanding how you deal with certain situations.

Building your confidence and learning how to be assertive can help with this. Sometimes, people will try to make you join in with activities which are not safe. Remember that taking foolish risks, particularly in response to a dare or because you want to show off, can have very serious consequences. You may want to think about how you have handled situations in the past, and consider the things you can do or say in the future to make sure you stay safe

Adults can also help by taking practical safety measures, such as fitting smoke alarms and door chains. They can also be available for young people to talk to, if they have any particular concerns about their physical or emotional safety.

Feeling secure and being safe allow you to enjoy yourself to the full.

Adults and children who have read this book together may like to discuss their feelings about the issues involved. Anybody who would like to talk to someone else about any aspect of personal safety might want to contact one of the organisations listed below. They should be able to offer practical advice, as well as support and information.

ROYAL SOCIETY FOR THE PREVENTION OF ACCIDENTS (ROSPA)
Cannon House, The Priory
Queensway
Birmingham B4 6BS
Tel: 0121 200 2461

ROSPA, SCOTLAND
Slateford House
53 Lanark Road
Edinburgh EH14 1TL
Tel: 0131 4557457

NSPCC
42 Curtain Road
London EC2A 3NH
Tel: 0800 800500 (24hr helpline)

THE CHILDREN'S SOCIETY
Margery Street
London WC1X 0JL
Tel: 0171 837 4299

CHILDLINE
2nd Floor, Royal Mail Building
Studd Street
London N1 0BR
Tel: 0171 239 1000
Tel: 0800 1111 (helpline)

KIDSCAPE
152 Buckingham Palace Road
London SW1W 9TR
Tel: 0171 730 3300

CHILD ACCIDENT PREVENTION TRUST
4th Floor, Clerks Court
18-20 Farringdon Lane
London EC1R 3AU
Tel: 0171 608 3828

NATIONAL CHILDREN'S BUREAU
8 Wakley Street
London EC1V 7QE
Tel: 0171 278 9441

DEPARTMENT OF HEALTH
Richmond House
79 Whitehall
London SW1A 2NS
Tel: 0800 665544 (health information service)
Tel: 0800 555777 (health literature line)

NATIONAL YOUTH FOUNDATION
P.O. Box 606
Carlingford
New South Wales 2118
Australia
Tel: 00 612 211 1788

THE MINISTRY OF YOUTH
PO Box 10–300
Wellington
New Zealand
Tel: 00 644 471 2158

Index

Photocredits

All the pictures in this book are by Roger Vlitos apart from: pages 17, Eye Ubiqutious;
page 26, Frank Spooner Pictures. The publishers wish to acknowledge that all the
people photographed in this book are models.